COME AND PRAISE

Compiled by Geoffrey Marshall-Taylor
Arrangements by Douglas Coombes

BBC

© BBC 1978
First published 1978
Fifteenth impression 1997
Sixteenth and seventeenth impressions 1998
Eighteenth impression 1999
Nineteenth impression 2000
Twentieth impression 2001
Twenty-first impression 2002
Twenty-second impression 2003
Published by BBC Educational Publishing, BBC White City,
201 Wood Lane, London W12 7TS.
Printed in England by Clays Ltd, St Ives plc
ISBN 0 563 32067 2

Acknowledgement is due to the following for permission to reprint the words of the hymns:

E. Bird, 30: P. Booth, 12: Celebration Services (International) Ltd, 32, 1971, 1975. All rights reserved. Used by permission: Chappell & Co Ltd, 61, assigned from Bradbury Wood Ltd 1972 for all countries of the world: H. Charlton, 60: Curwen Edition, 7: David Higham Associates Ltd, 1, on behalf of Eleanor Farjeon: T. Dudley-Smith, 9, 67: Herald Music Service, 70: High-Fye Music Ltd, 8/9 Frith St, London W1. Used by permission. All rights reserved, 18, 45: Lorna Music Co. Ltd, 69, 1967 reproduced with permission: G. Marshall-Taylor, 24, 26, 31, 49: Meyhew-McCrimmon Ltd, 4, 14, 53: T. McGuinness, 57, 59: Thankyou Music, P.O. Box 75, Eastbourne, East Sussex BN23 6NW, UK, 55, on behalf of McClellan/Pac/Ryecroft © 1974. Used by permission. Oxford University Press, 36, from *Songs of Praise,* 23, 50, 52, 62, from *Enlarged Songs of Praise;* 44, from *English Hymnal:* M. Payton, 5: J. Harvey, 29 (W & M): TRO Essex Music Ltd, 71: Salvationist Publishing and Supplies Ltd, 15, by permission of the International Music Board of the Salvation Army: Michael Saward, 6: Arthur Scholey, 72, 1978 from *Singalive* published by Collins: Scripture Union, 63, adapted by permission from *Sing to God* Hymn No. 102 'Spirit of God, unseen as the wind': Anthony Sheil Associates Ltd, 66: Stainer & Bell Ltd, 13, 1971 from *The Song of Caedmon;* 16. 1977 from *Christian Aid Songbook;* 17, 1969 from *New Orbit;* 22, 1963 from *Green Print for Song;* 28, 1964 from *New Orbit;* 42, 1969 from *New Orbit;* 47, 1971 from *Riding a Tune;* 65, 1965 from *New Life:* C. Strover, 2: Josef Weinberger Ltd, 25; 1965 from *Twenty-seven 20th Century Hymns;* 33, 1973 from *Teach Me How to Look;* 39, 1965 from *Twenty-seven 20th Century Hymns;* 58, 1960 from *Thirty 20th Century Hymn Tunes.* The BBC holds the copyright of 27.

Adaptations to 21, 24, 32, 49, 57, 63 are by G. Marshall-Taylor

Contents

THE CREATED WORLD

1 Morning has broken
2 Water of life
3 All things bright and beautiful
4 Autumn days
5 Somebody greater
6 The earth is yours, O God
7 All creatures of our God and King
8 Let us with a gladsome mind
9 Fill your hearts with joy
10 God who made the earth
11 For the beauty of the earth
12 Who put the colours in the rainbow?
13 Song of Caedmon
14 All the nations of the earth
15 God knows me
16 When God made the garden of creation
17 Think of a world without any flowers
18 He made me
19 He's got the whole world
20 Come, my brothers, praise the Lord

THE LIFE OF JESUS

21 Come and praise the Lord our King
22 Lord of the dance
23 Jesus good above all other
24 Go, tell it on the mountain
25 When Jesus walked in Galilee
26 Jesus Christ is here
27 A man for all the people
28 Judas and Mary
29 From the darkness came light

PRAISE AND THANKSGIVING

30 Join with us
31 God has promised
32 Thank you, Lord
33 Praise the Lord in everything
34 Praise to the Lord
35 Praise the Lord, you heavens

36 God is love
37 O praise ye the Lord!
38 Now thank we all our God
39 O Lord, all the world belongs to you
40 Praise him
41 Fill thou my life

THE JOURNEY OF LIFE
42 Travel on
43 Give me oil in my lamp
44 He who would valiant be
45 The journey of life
46 My faith, it is an oaken staff
47 One more step
48 Father, hear the prayer we offer
49 We are climbing
50 When a knight won his spurs

LIVING FOR GOD
51 The Lord's Prayer
52 Lord of all hopefulness
53 Peace, perfect peace
54 The King of love
55 Light up the fire
56 The Lord's my shepherd
57 Lost and found
58 At the name of Jesus
59 The best gift
60 I listen and I listen
61 The building song
62 Heavenly Father
63 Spirit of God
64 The wise may bring their learning

THE FAMILY OF MAN
65 When I needed a neighbour
66 In Christ there is no east or west
67 Black and white
68 Kum ba yah
69 The family of man
70 Cross over the road
71 If I had a hammer
72 A living song

1 Morning has broken,
   Like the first morning,
   Blackbird has spoken
   Like the first bird.
   Praise for the singing!
   Praise for the morning!
   Praise for them, springing
   Fresh from the Word!

2 Sweet the rain's new fall
   Sunlit from heaven,
   Like the first dewfall
   On the first grass.
   Praise for the sweetness
   Of the wet garden,
   Sprung in completeness
   Where his feet pass.

3 Mine is the sunlight!
   Mine is the morning
   Born of the one light
   Eden saw play!
   Praise with elation,
   Praise every morning,
   God's re-creation
   Of the new day!
                  Eleanor Farjeon

1 Have you heard the raindrops drumming on the
   roof-tops?
   Have you heard the raindrops dripping on the
   ground?
   Have you heard the raindrops splashing in the
   streams and running to the rivers all around?

   Chorus:
   There's water, water of life,
   Jesus gives us the water of life;
   There's water, water of life,
   Jesus gives us the water of life.

7

2 There's a busy workman digging in the desert,
  Digging with a spade that flashes in the sun;
  Soon there will be water rising in the wellshaft,
  spilling from the bucket as it comes.
  Chorus

3 Nobody can live who hasn't any water,
  When the land is dry then nothing much grows;
  Jesus gives us life if we drink the living water,
  sing it so that everybody knows.
  Chorus

                                    Christian Strover

Chorus:
All things bright and beautiful,
All creatures great and small,
All things wise and wonderful,
The Lord God made them all.

1 Each little flower that opens,
  Each little bird that sings,
  He made their glowing colours,
  He made their tiny wings:
  Chorus

2 The purple-headed mountain,
  The river running by,
  The sunset and the morning,
  That brightens up the sky:
  Chorus

3 The cold wind in the winter,
  The pleasant summer sun,
  The ripe fruits in the garden,
  He made them every one:
  Chorus

4 He gave us eyes to see them,
  And lips that we might tell
  How great is God Almighty,
  Who has made all things well:
  Chorus

                          Cecil Frances Alexander

1 Autumn days when the grass is jewelled
  And the silk inside a chestnut shell,
  Jet planes meeting in the air to be refuelled,
  All these things I love so well.

  Chorus:
  So I mustn't forget.
  No, I mustn't forget,
  To say a great big thank-you,
  I mustn't forget.

2 Clouds that look like familiar faces,
  And a winter's moon with frosted rings,
  Smell of bacon as I fasten up my laces,
  And the song the milkman sings.
  Chorus

3 Whipped-up spray that is rainbow-scattered,
  And a swallow curving in the sky.
  Shoes so comfy though they're worn-out and
  they're battered,
  And the taste of apple-pie.
  Chorus

4 Scent of gardens when the rain's been falling,
  And a minnow darting down a stream,
  Picked-up engine that's been stuttering and
  stalling,
  And a win for my home team.
  Chorus

                                    Estelle White

1 Carpenter, carpenter, make me a tree,
  That's the work of somebody far greater
  than me;
  Gardener, gardener, shape me a flower,
  That's the work of somebody with far greater
  power.

9

Chorus:
Somebody greater than you or me,
Put the apple on the apple tree;
The flower in the earth and the fish in the sea,
Are by somebody greater than you or me.

2 Builder, now raise up a coloured rainbow,
  That's something far greater than people could
  know;
  Farmer, I ask you, design me some corn,
  That's somebody greater than any man born.
  Chorus

3 Now, electrician, will you light a star,
  That's the work of somebody who's greater
  by far;
  Plumber, connect up the river and sea,
  That's the work of somebody far greater
  than me.
  Chorus

                                      Marion Payton

1 The earth is yours, O God,
  You nourish it with rain;
  The streams and rivers overflow,
  The land bears seeds again.

2 The soil is yours, O God,
  The shoots are moist with dew,
  And, ripened by the burning sun,
  The corn grows straight and true.

3 The hills are yours, O God,
  Their grass is lush and green,
  Providing pastures for the flocks,
  Which everywhere are seen.

4 The whole rich land is yours,
  For fodder or for plough,
  And so, for rain, sun, soil and seed,
  O God, we thank you now.
                          Michael Saward

1 All creatures of our God and King,
Lift up your voice and with us sing,
Alleluia, Alleluia!
You burning sun with golden beam,
You silver moon with softer gleam,

Chorus:
O praise Him, O praise Him,
Alleluia, Alleluia, Alleluia!

2 You rushing wind who are so strong,
You clouds that sail in heaven along,
O praise Him, Alleluia!
You rising morn, in praise rejoice,
You lights of evening, find a voice.
Chorus

3 You flowing water, pure and clear,
Make music for your Lord to hear,
Alleluia, Alleluia!
You fire so masterful and bright,
Who gives to man both warmth and light,
Chorus

4 Let all things their Creator bless,
And worship Him in humbleness,
O praise Him, Alleluia!
Praise, praise the Father, praise the Son,
And praise the Spirit, Three in One.
Chorus

William Draper

1 Let us with a gladsome mind
Praise the Lord, for He is kind:

Chorus:
For His mercies still endure,
Ever faithful, ever sure.

2 Let us blaze His name abroad,
For of gods He is the God:
Chorus

3 He, with all-commanding might,
Filled the new-made world with light:
Chorus

4 All things living He does feed,
His full hand supplies their need:
Chorus

5 Let us with gladsome mind
Praise the Lord, for He is kind:
Chorus

John Milton

1 Fill your hearts with joy and gladness,
Sing and praise your God and mine!
Great the Lord in love and wisdom,
Might and majesty divine!
He who framed the starry heavens
Knows and names them as they shine.

2 Praise the Lord for times and seasons,
Cloud and sunshine, wind and rain;
Spring to melt the snows of winter
Till the waters flow again;
Grass upon the mountain pastures,
Golden valleys thick with grain.

3 Fill your hearts with joy and gladness,
Peace and plenty crown your days;
Love His laws, declare His judgements,
Walk in all His words and ways,
He the Lord and we His children;
Praise the Lord, all people, praise!

Timothy Dudley-Smith

• *Repeat the last line of each verse for Tune 2.*

1 God who made the earth,
The air, the sky, the sea,
Who gave the light its birth,
Careth for me.

12

2 God who made the grass,
   The flower, the fruit, the tree,
   The day and night to pass,
   Careth for me.

3 God who made the sun,
   The moon, the stars, is He
   Who, when life's clouds come on,
   Careth for me.
                                    Sarah Rhodes

1 For the beauty of the earth,
   For the beauty of the skies,
   For the love which from our birth
   Over and around us lies,
   Father, unto Thee we raise
   This our sacrifice of praise.

2 For the beauty of each hour
   Of the day and of the night,
   Hill and vale and tree and flower,
   Sun and moon and stars of light,
   Father, unto Thee we raise
   This our sacrifice of praise.

3 For the joy of human love,
   Brother, sister, parent, child,
   Friends on earth and friends above,
   For all gentle thoughts and mild,
   Father, unto Thee we raise
   This our sacrifice of praise.

4 For each perfect gift of Thine
   To our race so freely given,
   Graces human and divine,
   Flowers of earth and buds of heaven,
   Father, unto Thee we raise
   This our sacrifice of praise.
                                    Folliott Pierpoint

1 Who put the colours in the rainbow?
Who put the salt into the sea?
Who put the cold into the snowflake?
Who made you and me?
Who put the hump upon the camel?
Who put the neck on the giraffe?
Who put the tail upon the monkey?
Who made hyenas laugh?
Who made whales and snails and quails?
Who made hogs and dogs and frogs?
Who made bats and rats and cats?
Who made everything?

2 Who put the gold into the sunshine?
Who put the sparkle in the stars?
Who put the silver in the moonlight?
Who made Earth and Mars?
Who put the scent into the roses?
Who taught the honey bee to dance?
Who put the tree inside the acorn?
It surely can't be chance!
Who made seas and leaves and trees?
Who made snow and winds that blow?
Who made streams and rivers flow?
God made all of these!

Paul Booth

1 Oh praise Him!
Oh praise Him!
Oh praise Him!
Oh praise Him!
Oh praise Him!
Oh praise Him!
He made the heavens, He made our sky,
The sun, the moon, the stars on high.
He formed our world, His mighty hand
Divided sea and land.
He moves in wind and rain and snow,
His life is in all things that grow.
Oh praise Him!
Oh praise Him!
Oh praise Him!

2 Oh praise Him!
  Oh praise Him!
  Oh praise Him!
  Oh praise Him!
  Oh praise Him!
  Oh praise Him!
  His joy is in the eagle's flight,
  The tiger's roar, the lion's might
  The lamb, the python and the whale,
  The spider, ant and snail.
  All things that leap and swim and fly
  On land and sea and in the sky,
  They praise Him,
  They praise Him,
  They praise Him.

3 Oh praise Him!
  Oh praise Him!
  Oh praise Him!
  Oh praise Him!
  Oh praise Him!
  Oh praise Him!
  He lives His life in love and joy
  In man and woman, girl and boy.
  His purpose is in me and you,
  In what we are and do.
  His love is in us when we sing
  With every God-created thing,
  And praise Him,
  And praise Him,
  And praise Him.

Arthur Scholey

14

Chorus:
All the nations of the earth,
Praise the Lord who brings to birth
The greatest star, the smallest flower:
Alleluia.

1 Let the heavens praise the Lord:
  Alleluia.
  Moon and stars, praise the Lord:
  Alleluia.
  Chorus

2 Snow-capped mountains, praise the Lord:
  Alleluia.
  Moon and stars, praise the Lord:
  Alleluia.
  Chorus

3 Deep sea-water, praise the Lord:
  Alleluia.
  Gentle rain, praise the Lord:
  Alleluia.
  Chorus

4 Roaring lion, praise the Lord:
  Alleluia.
  Singing birds, praise the Lord:
  Alleluia.
  Chorus

5 Kings and princes, praise the Lord:
  Alleluia.
  Young and old, praise the Lord:
  Alleluia.
  Chorus

Michael Cockett

1 There are hundreds of sparrows, thousands,
  millions,
  They're two a penny, far too many there
  must be;
  There are hundreds and thousands,
  millions of sparrows,
  But God knows every-one and God knows me.

2 There are hundreds of flowers, thousands,
  millions,
  And flowers fair the meadows wear for all
  to see;
  There are hundreds and thousands,
  millions of flowers,
  But God knows every-one and God knows me.

3 There are hundreds of planets, thousands,
  millions,
  Way out in space each has a place by
  God's decree;
  There are hundreds and thousands,
  millions of planets,
  But God knows every-one and God knows me.

4 There are hundreds of children, thousands,
  millions,
  And yet their names are written on
  God's memory,
  There are hundreds and thousands,
  millions of children,
  But God knows every-one and God knows me!

John Gowans

16

1 When God made the garden of creation,
He filled it full of His love;
When God made the garden of creation,
He saw that it was good.
There's room for you,
And room for me,
And room for everyone:
For God is a Father, who loves His children,
And gives them a place in the sun.
When God made the garden of creation,
He filled it full of His love.

2 When God made the hamper of creation,
He filled it full of His love;
When God made the hamper of creation,
He saw that it was good.
There's food for you,
And food for me,
And food for everyone:
But man is so greedy and wastes God's bounty,
That some won't get any at all.
When God made the hamper of creation,
He filled it full of His love.

3 When God made the family of creation,
He made it out of His love;
When God made the family of creation,
He saw that it was good.
There's love for you,
And love for me,
And love for everyone:
But man is so selfish, ignores his neighbour,
And seeks his own place in the sun.
When God made the family of creation,
He made it out of His love.

4 When God made the garden of creation,
He filled it full of His love;
When God made the garden of creation,
He saw that it was good.
There's room for you,
And room for me,
And room for everyone:

18

For God is a Father, who loves His children,
And gives them a place in the sun.
When God made the garden of creation,
He filled it full of His love.

Paul Booth

1 Think of a world without any flowers,
Think of a world without any trees,
Think of a sky without any sunshine,
Think of the air without any breeze.
We thank you, Lord, for flowers and trees and sunshine,
We thank you, Lord, and praise your holy name.

2 Think of a world without any animals,
Think of a field without any herd,
Think of a stream without any fishes,
Think of a dawn without any bird.
We thank you, Lord, for all your living creatures,
We thank you, Lord, and praise your holy name.

3 Think of a world without any people,
Think of a street with no-one living there,
Think of a town without any houses,
No-one to love and nobody to care.
We thank you, Lord, for families and friendships,
We thank you, Lord, and praise your holy name.

Doreen Newport

1 He gave me eyes so I could see
The wonders of the world;
Without my eyes I could not see
The other boys and girls.
He gave me ears so I could hear
The wind and rain and sea.
I've got to tell it to the world,
He made me.

2 He gave me lips so I could speak
And say what's in my mind;
Without my lips I could not speak
A single word or line.
He made my mind so I could think,
And choose what I should be.
I've got to tell it to the world,
He made me.

3 He gave me hands so I could touch,
And hold a thousand things;
I need my hands to help me write,
To help me fetch and bring.
These feet He made so I could run,
He meant me to be free.
I've got to tell it to the world,
He made me.

Alan Pinnock

Chorus:
He's got the whole world, in His hand,
He's got the whole wide world, in His hand,
He's got the whole world, in His hand,
He's got the whole world in His hand.

1 He's got the wind and the rain, in His hand,
He's got the wind and the rain, in His hand,
He's got the wind and the rain, in His hand,
He's got the whole world in His hand.
Chorus

2 He's got the sun and the moon, in His hand,
  He's got the sun and the moon, in His hand,
  He's got the sun and the moon, in His hand,
  He's got the whole world in His hand.
  Chorus

3 He's got the plants and the creatures,
    in His hand,
  He's got the plants and the creatures,
    in His hand,
  He's got the plants and the creatures,
    in His hand,
  He's got the whole world in His hand.
  Chorus

4 He's got everybody here, in His hand,
  He's got everybody here, in His hand,
  He's got everybody here, in His hand,
  He's got the whole world in His hand.
  Chorus

                              Traditional

1 Come, my brothers, praise the Lord, alleluia.
  He's our God and we are His, alleluia.

2 Come to Him with songs of praise, alleluia.
  Songs of praise, rejoice in Him, alleluia.

3 For the Lord is a mighty God, alleluia.
  He is King of all the world, alleluia.

4 In His hands are valleys deep, alleluia.
  In His hands are mountain peaks, alleluia.

5 In His hands are all the seas, alleluia.
  And the lands which He has made, alleluia.

6 Come, my brothers, praise the Lord, alleluia.
  He's our God and we are His, alleluia.

                              Traditional

Chorus:
Come and praise the Lord our King, Hallelujah,
Come and praise the Lord our King, Hallelujah.

1 Christ was born in Bethlehem, Hallelujah,
Son of God and Son of Man, Hallelujah.
Chorus

2 From him love and wisdom came, Hallelujah;
All his life was free from blame, Hallelujah.
Chorus

3 Jesus died at Calvary, Hallelujah,
Rose again triumphantly, Hallelujah.
Chorus

4 He will be with us today, Hallelujah,
And forever with us stay, Hallelujah.
Chorus

Traditional (adapted)

1 I danced in the morning
When the world was begun,
And I danced in the moon
And the stars and the sun;
And I came down from heaven
And I danced on the earth;
At Bethlehem
I had my birth.

Chorus:
Dance then, wherever you may be,
I am the Lord of the Dance, said he,
And I'll lead you all wherever you may be,
And I'll lead you all in the dance, said he.

2 I danced for the scribe
And the pharisee,
But they would not dance
And they wouldn't follow me.

I danced for the fishermen,
For James and John —
They came with me
And the dance went on.
Chorus

3 I danced on the Sabbath
And I cured the lame;
The holy people
Said it was a shame.
They whipped and they stripped
And they hung me on high,
And they left me there
On a cross to die.
Chorus

4 They cut me down
And I leapt up high;
I am the life
That'll never, never die.
I'll live in you
If you live in me;
I am the Lord
Of the Dance, said he.
Chorus

                                    Sydney Carter

1 Jesus, good above all other,
Gentle child of gentle mother,
In a stable born our brother,
Give us grace to persevere.

2 Jesus, cradled in a manger,
For us facing every danger,
Living as a homeless stranger,
We make you our King most dear.

3 Jesus, for your people dying,
Risen Master, death defying,
Lord in heaven, your grace supplying,
Keep us to your presence near.

4 Lord, in all our doings guide us,
  Pride and hate shall ne'er divide us,
  We'll go on with you beside us,
  And with joy we'll persevere!
                    Percy Dearmer

Chorus:
Go, tell it on the mountain,
Over the hills and everywhere;
Go, tell it on the mountain
That Jesus is his name.

1 He possessed no riches, no home to lay his head;
  He saw the needs of others and cared for them
  instead.
  Chorus

2 He reached out and touched them, the blind,
  the deaf, the lame;
  He spoke and listened gladly to anyone
  who came.
  Chorus

3 Some turned away in anger, with hatred in
  the eye;
  They tried him and condemned him, then led
  him out to die.
  Chorus

4 'Father, now forgive them' — those were the
  words he said;
  In three more days he was alive and risen from
  the dead.
  Chorus

5 He still comes to people, his life moves through
  the lands;
  He uses us for speaking, he touches with
  our hands.
  Chorus

                  Geoffrey Marshall-Taylor

1 When Jesus walked in Galilee,
  He gave all men a chance to see
  What God intended them to be,
  And how they ought to live.

2 When Jesus hung upon the cross,
  Enduring hunger, pain and loss,
  He looked, with loving eyes, across
  The scene, and said, 'Forgive.'

3 When Jesus rose on Easter Day,
  He met a woman in the way
  And said, 'Go to my friends, and say
  The Master is alive.'

4 When Jesus comes to us each day,
  And listens to us as we pray,
  We'll listen too, and hear him say,
  'Come, follow me, and live!'

John Glandfield

1 There is singing in the desert,
    there is laughter in the skies,
  There are wise men filled with wonder,
    there are shepherds with surprise,
  You can tell the world is dancing
    by the light that's in their eyes,
  For Jesus Christ is here.

Chorus:
Come and sing aloud your praises,
Come and sing aloud your praises,
Come and sing aloud your praises,
For Jesus Christ is here.

2 He hears deaf men by the lakeside,
    he sees blind men in the streets,
He goes up to those who cannot walk,
    he talks to all he meets,
Touching silken robes or tattered clothes,
    it's everyone he greets,
For Jesus Christ is here.
Chorus

3 There is darkness on the hillside,
    there is sorrow in the town,
There's a man upon a wooden cross,
    a man who's gazing down,
You can see the marks of love
    and not the furrows of a frown,
For Jesus Christ is here.
Chorus

4 There is singing in the desert,
    there is laughter in the skies,
There are wise men filled with wonder,
    there are shepherds with surprise,
You can tell the world is dancing
    by the light that's in their eyes,
For Jesus Christ is here.
Chorus

                            Geoffrey Marshall-Taylor

27

1 There's a child in the streets
Gives joy to all he meets,
Full of life, with many friends,
Works and plays till daylight ends.

Chorus:
There's a man for all the people,
A man whose love is true.
May this man for all the people
Help me love others too.

2 There's a preacher in a crowd
   Shouts to fishermen out loud,
   'Leave your boats and leave the sea,
   Come along and work with me.'
   Chorus

3 There's a teacher tells a tale,
   Makes men argue without fail,
   Some are angry, some agree,
   When he says, 'You follow me.'
   Chorus

4 There's a leader at a feast,
   But he says that he's the least,
   Rolls his sleeves to wash their feet,
   Breaks the bread and tells them, 'Eat.'
   Chorus

5 There's a prisoner on a cross
   And his friends weep for their loss,
   But a soldier with a sword
   Says, 'This man has come from God.'
   Chorus

6 There's a voice inside a room,
   'I have risen from the tomb,
   I am bringing you God's peace
   And your joy will never cease.'
   Chorus

                           Geoffrey Curtis

1 Said Judas to Mary,
   'Now what will you do
   With your ointment
   So rich and so rare?'
   'I'll pour it all over
   The feet of the Lord,
   And I'll wipe it away with my hair,'
   She said,
   'I'll wipe it away with my hair.'

2 'Oh Mary, oh Mary,
   Oh think of the poor —
   This ointment, it
   Could have been sold.
   And think of the blankets
   And think of the bread
   You could buy with the silver and gold,'
   He said,
   'You could buy with the silver and gold.'

3 'Tomorrow, tomorrow,
   I'll think of the poor,
   Tomorrow,' she said,
   'Not today.
   For dearer than all
   Of the poor in the world
   Is my love who is going away,'
   She said,
   'My love who is going away.'

4 Said Jesus to Mary,
   'Your love is so deep
   Today you may do
   As you will.
   Tomorrow you say
   I am going away,
   But my body I leave with you still,'
   He said,
   'My body I leave with you still.'

5 'The poor of the world
   Are my body,' he said,
   'To the end of the world
   They shall be.
   The bread and the blankets
   You give to the poor
   You'll find you have given to me,'
   He said,
   'You'll find you have given to me.'

6 'My body will hang
   On the cross of the world
   Tomorrow,' he said,
   'And today,

And Martha and Mary
Will find me again
And wash all my sorrow away,'
He said,
'And wash all my sorrow away.'

Sydney Carter

29

Chorus:
From the darkness came light,
From the blackest of nights;
Wait for the morning, the sunlight, the dawning;
From the darkness came light.

1 Earth so dark and so cold, what great secrets
   you hold;
   The promise of spring, the wonder you bring
   The beauty of nature unfolds.
   Chorus

2 Jesus was born in a stall, born to bring light
   to us all.
   He came to love us, a new life to give us;
   Jesus was born in a stall.
   Chorus

3 Jesus died on Calvary, suffered for you and me;
   He rose from the dark and gloom,
   out of a stony tomb,
   Walked in the world and was free.
   Chorus

4 We have this new life to share, a love to pass
   on everywhere;
   Time spent in giving, a joy in our living,
   In showing to others we care.
   Chorus

Jancis Harvey

Chorus:
Join with us to sing God's praises,
For His love and for His care,
For the happiness He gives us,
Praise Him for the world we share.

1 Thank Him for the town and country,
Thank Him for the sun and rain,
Thank Him for our homes and gardens,
Sing His praises once again.
Chorus

2 We have eyes to look around us,
We have strength to work and play,
We have voices we can use — to
Sing His praises every day.
Chorus

3 Praise Him in your words of kindness,
Praise Him helping those in need,
Praise Him in your thought for others,
Sing His praises with each deed.
Chorus

Edna Bird

1 Can you be sure that the rain will fall?
Can you be sure that birds will fly?
Can you be sure that rivers will flow?
Or that the sun will light the sky?

Chorus:
God has promised.
God never breaks a promise He makes.
His word is always true.

2 Can you be sure that the tide will turn?
Can you be sure that grass will grow?
Can you be sure that night will come,
Or that the sun will melt the snow?
Chorus

3 You can be sure that God is near;
  You can be sure He won't let you down;
  You can be sure He'll always hear;
  And that He's given Jesus, His Son.
  Chorus

                    Geoffrey Marshall-Taylor

1 Thank you, Lord, for this new day,
  Thank you, Lord, for this new day,
  Thank you, Lord, for this new day,
  Right where we are.

  Chorus:
  Alleluia, praise the Lord,
  Alleluia, praise the Lord,
  Alleluia, praise the Lord,
  Right where we are.

2 Thank you, Lord, for food to eat,
  Thank you, Lord, for food to eat,
  Thank you, Lord, for food to eat,
  Right where we are.
  Chorus

3 Thank you, Lord, for clothes to wear,
  Thank you, Lord, for clothes to wear,
  Thank you, Lord, for clothes to wear,
  Right where we are.
  Chorus

4 Thank you, Lord, for all your gifts,
  Thank you, Lord, for all your gifts,
  Thank you, Lord, for all your gifts,
  Right where we are.
  Chorus

  Diane Andrew
  adapted by Geoffrey Marshall-Taylor

1 Praise the Lord in the rhythm of your music,
Praise the Lord in the freedom of your dance,
Praise the Lord in the country and the city,
Praise Him in the living of your life!

2 Praise the Lord on the organ and piano,
Praise the Lord on guitar and on the drums,
Praise the Lord on the tambourine and cymbals,
Praise Him in the singing of your song!

3 Praise the Lord with the movement of your
bodies,
Praise the Lord with the clapping of your hands,
Praise the Lord with your poetry and painting,
Praise Him in the acting of your play!

4 Praise the Lord in the feeding of the hungry,
Praise the Lord in the healing of disease,
Praise the Lord as you show His love in action,
Praise Him in your caring for the poor!

5 Praise the Lord, every nation, every people,
Praise the Lord, men and women, old and
young,
Praise the Lord, let us celebrate together,
Praise Him everything in heaven and earth!

Peter Casey

1 Praise to the Lord, the Almighty,
the King of creation;
O my soul, praise Him, for He is thy
health and salvation;
All ye who hear,
Brothers and sisters draw near,
Praise Him in glad adoration.

2 Praise to the Lord, who o'er all things
so wondrously reigneth;
Shelters thee under His wings, yea,
so gently sustaineth;
Hast thou not seen?
All that is needful hath been
Granted in what He ordaineth.

3 Praise to the Lord, who doth prosper thy work
and defend thee;
Surely his goodness and mercy
will daily attend thee;
Ponder anew
What the Almighty can do,
He who with love doth befriend thee.

4 Praise to the Lord! O let all that is in me
adore Him.
All that hath life and breath, come now
with praises before Him!
Let the Amen
Sound from His people again:
Gladly for aye we adore Him.
Joachim Neander, trans. Catherine Winkworth

1 Praise the Lord! you heavens, adore Him;
Praise Him, angels, in the height;
Sun and moon, rejoice before Him,
Praise Him, all you stars and light:
Praise the Lord! for He has spoken,
Worlds His mighty voice obeyed;
Laws, which never shall be broken,
For their guidance He has made.

2 Praise the Lord! for He is glorious;
Never shall His promise fail;
God has made His saints victorious,
Sin and death shall not prevail.
Praise the God of our salvation;
Hosts on high, His power proclaim;
Heaven and earth, and all creation,
Laud and magnify His name!
Foundling Hospital Collection

36

1 God is love; His the care,
Tending each, everywhere.
God is love — all is there!
Jesus came to show Him,
That mankind might know Him:

Chorus:
Sing aloud, loud, loud!
Sing aloud, loud, loud!
God is good! God is truth!
God is beauty! Praise Him!

2 None can see God above;
All have here man to love;
Thus may we Godward move,
Finding him in others,
Holding all men brothers:
Chorus

3 Jesus lived here for men,
Strove and died, rose again,
Rules our hearts, now as then;
For he came to save us
By the truth he gave us:
Chorus

4 To our Lord praise we sing —
Light and life, friend and king,
Coming down love to bring,
Pattern for our duty,
Showing God in beauty:
Chorus

Percy Dearmer

37

1 O praise ye the Lord!
Praise Him in the height;
Rejoice in His word,
Ye angels of light;
Ye heavens, adore Him,
By whom ye were made,
And worship before Him,
In brightness arrayed.

34

2 O praise ye the Lord!
  All things that give sound;
  Each jubilant chord,
  Re-echo around;
  Loud organs, His glory
  Forth tell in deep tone,
  And sweet harp, the story,
  Of what He hath done.

3 O praise ye the Lord!
  Thanksgiving and song
  To Him be outpoured
  All ages along;
  For love in creation,
  For heaven restored,
  For grace of salvation,
  O praise ye the Lord!
               Sir Henry Baker

1 Now thank we all our God,
  With heart and hands and voices,
  Who wondrous things has done,
  In whom His world rejoices;
  Who, from our mothers' arms,
  Has blessed us on our way
  With countless gifts of love,
  And still is ours today.

2 O may this bounteous God
  Through all our life be near us,
  With ever-joyful hearts
  And blessed peace to cheer us,
  And keep us in His grace,
  And guide us when perplexed,
  And free us from all ills
  In this world and the next.

3 All praise and thanks to God
   The Father now be given,
   The Son, and Him who reigns
   With Them in highest heaven;
   The one, eternal God,
   Whom earth and heaven adore;
   For thus it was, is now,
   And shall be ever more.

   Martin Rinkart, trans. Catherine Winkworth

1 O Lord, all the world belongs to you,
   And you are always making all things new.
   What is wrong you forgive,
   And the new life you give
   Is what's turning the world upside down.

2 The world's only loving to its friends,
   But your way of loving never ends,
   Loving enemies too;
   And this loving with you,
   Is what's turning the world upside down.

3 The world lives divided and apart,
   You draw men together, and we start
   In our friendship to see
   That in harmony we
   Can be turning the world upside down.

4 The world wants the wealth to live in state,
   But you show a new way to be great:
   Like a servant you came,
   And if we do the same,
   We'll be turning the world upside down.

5 O Lord, all the world belongs to you,
   And you are always making all things new.
   What is wrong you forgive,
   And the new life you give
   Is what's turning the world upside down.
                              Patrick Appleford

1 Praise Him, praise Him,
   Praise Him in the morning,
   Praise Him in the noon-time,
   Praise Him, praise Him,
   Praise Him when the sun goes down.

2 Trust Him, trust Him,
   Trust Him in the morning,
   Trust Him in the noon-time,
   Trust Him, trust Him,
   Trust Him when the sun goes down.

3 Serve Him, serve Him,
   Serve Him in the morning,
   Serve Him in the noon-time,
   Serve Him, serve Him,
   Serve Him when the sun goes down.

4 Praise Him, praise Him,
   Praise Him in the morning,
   Praise Him in the noon-time,
   Praise Him, praise Him,
   Praise Him when the sun goes down.
                              Traditional

1 Fill thou my life, O Lord my God,
   In every part with praise,
   That my whole being may proclaim
   Thy being and thy ways.

2 Not for the lip of praise alone,
   Nor e'en the praising heart,
   I ask, but for a life made up
   Of praise in every part:

3 Praise in the common things of life,
   Its goings out and in;
   Praise in each duty and each deed,
   However small and mean.

37

4 Fill every part of me with praise;
   Let all my being speak
   Of thee and of thy love, O Lord,
   Poor though I be and weak.

5 So shall no part of day or night
   From sacredness be free;
   But all my life, in every step,
   Be fellowship with thee.
                    Horatius Bonar

1 Travel on, travel on, there's a river that is
   flowing,
   A river that is flowing night and day.
   Travel on, travel on to the river that is flowing,
   The river will be with you all the way.
   Travel on, travel on to the river that is flowing,
   The river will be with you all the way.

2 Travel on, travel on, there's a flower that is
   growing,
   A flower that is growing night and day.
   Travel on, travel on to the flower that is
   growing,
   The flower will be with you all the way.
   Travel on, travel on to the flower that is
   growing,
   The flower will be with you all the way.

3 Travel on, travel on to the music that is playing,
   The music that is playing night and day.
   Travel on, travel on to the music that is playing,
   The music will be with you all the way.
   Travel on, travel on to the music that is playing,
   The music will be with you all the way.

4 In the kingdom of heaven is my end and my
  beginning
  And the road that I must follow night and day.
  Travel on, travel on to the kingdom that is
  coming,
  The kingdom will be with you all the way.
  Travel on, travel on to the kingdom that is
  coming,
  The kingdom will be with you all the way.

Sydney Carter

1 Give me oil in my lamp, keep me burning.
  Give me oil in my lamp, I pray.
  Give me oil in my lamp, keep me burning,
  Keep me burning till the break of day.

   Chorus:
   Sing hosanna, sing hosanna,
   Sing hosanna to the King of Kings!
   Sing hosanna, sing hosanna,
   Sing hosanna to the King!

2 Give me joy in my heart, keep me singing.
  Give me joy in my heart, I pray.
  Give me joy in my heart, keep me singing,
  Keep me singing till the break of day.
  Chorus

3 Give me love in my heart, keep me serving.
  Give me love in my heart, I pray.
  Give me love in my heart, keep me serving,
  Keep me serving till the break of day.
  Chorus

4 Give me peace in my heart, keep me resting.
  Give me peace in my heart, I pray.
  Give me peace in my heart, keep me resting,
  Keep me resting till the break of day.
  Chorus

Traditional

1 He who would valiant be
  'Gainst all disaster,
  Let him in constancy
  Follow the Master.
  There's no discouragement
  Shall make him once relent
  His first avowed intent
  To be a pilgrim.

2 Who so beset him round
  With dismal stories,
  Do but themselves confound —
  His strength the more is.
  No foes shall stay his might,
  Though he with giants fight:
  He will make good his right
  To be a pilgrim.

3 Since, Lord, thou dost defend
  Us with thy Spirit,
  We know we at the end
  Shall life inherit.
  Then fancies flee away!
  I'll fear not what men say,
  I'll labour night and day
  To be a pilgrim.

Percy Dearmer, adapted from John Bunyan

1 The journey of life
  May be easy, may be hard,
  There'll be danger on the way;
  With Christ at my side
  I'll do battle, as I ride,
  'Gainst the foe that would lead me astray:

Chorus:
Will you ride, ride, ride
With the King of Kings,
Will you follow my leader true;
Will you shout Hosanna
To the lowly Son of God,
Who died for me and you?

2 My burden is light
And a song is in my heart
As I travel on life's way;
For Christ is my Lord
And he's given me his word
That by my side he'll stay:
Chorus

Valerie Collison

1 My faith, it is an oaken staff,
The traveller's well-loved aid;
My faith, it is a weapon stout,
The soldier's trusty blade.
I'll travel on, and still be stirred
To action at my Master's word;
By all my perils undeterred,
A soldier unafraid.

2 My faith, it is an oaken staff,
O let me on it lean;
My faith, it is a trusty sword,
May falsehood find it keen.
Thy spirit, Lord, to me impart,
O make me what thou ever art,
Of patient and courageous heart,
As all true saints have been.

Thomas Lynch

47

1 One more step along the world I go,
    One more step along the world I go,
    From the old things to the new
    Keep me travelling along with you.

Chorus:
And it's from the old I travel to the new,
Keep me travelling along with you.

2 Round the corners of the world I turn,
    More and more about the world I learn.
    And the new things that I see
    You'll be looking at along with me.
    Chorus

3 As I travel through the bad and good
    Keep me travelling the way I should.
    Where I see no way to go
    You'll be telling me the way, I know.
    Chorus

4 Give me courage when the world is rough,
    Keep me loving though the world is tough.
    Leap and sing in all I do,
    Keep me travelling along with you.
    Chorus

5 You are older than the world can be
    You are younger than the life in me.
    Ever old and ever new,
    Keep me travelling along with you.
    Chorus

                                        Sydney Carter

1 Father, hear the prayer we offer:
Not for ease that prayer shall be,
But for strength that we may ever
Live our lives courageously.

2 Not for ever in green pastures
Do we ask our way to be;
But the steep and rugged pathway
May we tread rejoicingly.

3 Not for ever by still waters
Would we idly rest and stay;
But would smite the living fountains
From the rocks along our way.

4 Be our strength in hours of weakness,
In our wanderings be our guide;
Through endeavour, failure, danger,
Father, be thou at our side.

Love Willis

1 We are climbing Jesus' ladder, ladder,
We are climbing Jesus' ladder, ladder,
We are climbing Jesus' ladder, ladder,
Children of the Lord.

Chorus:
So let's all
Rise and shine and give God the glory, glory,
Rise and shine and give God the glory, glory,
Rise and shine and give God the glory, glory,
Children of the Lord.

2 We are following where he leads us, leads us,
We are following where he leads us, leads us,
We are following where he leads us, leads us,
Children of the Lord.
Chorus

3 We are reaching out to others, others,
  We are reaching out to others, others,
  We are reaching out to others, others,
  Children of the Lord.
  Chorus

4 We are one with all who serve Him, serve Him,
  We are one with all who serve Him, serve Him,
  We are one with all who serve Him, serve Him,
  Children of the Lord.
  Chorus

                              Traditional (adapted)

1 When a knight won his spurs in the stories of
  old,
  He was gentle and brave, he was gallant and
  bold;
  With a shield on his arm and a lance in his hand,
  For God and for valour he rode through the
  land.

2 No charger have I, and no sword by my side,
  Yet still to adventure and battle I ride,
  Though back into storyland giants have fled,
  And the knights are no more and the dragons
  are dead.

3 Let faith be my shield and let joy be my steed
  'Gainst the dragons of anger, the ogres of greed;
  And let me set free, with the sword of my youth,
  From the castle of darkness, the power of
  the truth.

                              Jan Struther

51 Our Father, who art in heaven,
Hallowed be thy name;
Thy kingdom come, thy will be done,
Hallowed be thy name,
On the earth as it is in heaven,
Hallowed be thy name.
Give us this day our daily bread,
Hallowed be thy name.
Forgive us all our trespasses,
Hallowed be thy name,
As we forgive those who trespass against us,
Hallowed be thy name;
And lead us not into temptation,
Hallowed be thy name,
But deliver us from all that is evil,
Hallowed be thy name;
For thine is the kingdom, the power and the glory,
Hallowed be thy name,
For ever and for ever and ever,
Hallowed be thy name.
Amen, Amen, it shall be so,
Hallowed be thy name;
Amen, Amen, it shall be so,
Hallowed be thy name.

Traditional Caribbean

52
1 Lord of all hopefulness, Lord of all joy,
Whose trust ever child-like, no cares
could destroy,
Be there at our waking, and give us, we pray,
Your bliss in our hearts, Lord, at the break
of the day.

2 Lord of all eagerness, Lord of all faith,
Whose strong hands were skilled at the plane
and the lathe,
Be there at our labours, and give us, we pray,
Your strength in our hearts, Lord, at the noon
cf the day.

3 Lord of all kindliness, Lord of all grace,
Your hands swift to welcome, your arms to
embrace,
Be there at our homing, and give us, we pray,
Your love in our hearts, Lord, at the eve
of the day.

4 Lord of all gentleness, Lord of all calm,
Whose voice is contentment, whose presence
is balm,
Be there at our sleeping, and give us, we pray,
Your peace in our hearts, Lord, at the end
of the day.

Jan Struther

1 Peace, perfect peace, is the gift of Christ
our Lord.
Peace, perfect peace, is the gift of Christ
our Lord.
Thus, says the Lord, will the world know
my friends,
Peace, perfect peace, is the gift of Christ
our Lord.

2 Hope, perfect hope, is the gift of Christ our Lord.
Hope, perfect hope, is the gift of Christ our Lord.
Thus, says the Lord, will the world know
my friends,
Hope, perfect hope, is the gift of Christ our Lord.

3 Joy, perfect joy, is the gift of Christ our Lord.
Joy, perfect joy, is the gift of Christ our Lord.
Thus, says the Lord, will the world know
my friends,
Joy, perfect joy, is the gift of Christ our Lord.

Kevin Mayhew

1 The King of love my shepherd is,
  Whose goodness faileth never;
  I nothing lack if I am His
  And He is mine for ever.

2 Where streams of living water flow
  My ransomed soul He leadeth,
  And where the verdant pastures grow
  With food celestial feedeth.

3 Perverse and foolish oft I strayed;
  But yet in love He sought me,
  And on His shoulder gently laid,
  And home rejoicing brought me.

4 In death's dark vale I fear no ill,
  With thee, dear Lord, beside me;
  Thy rod and staff my comfort still,
  Thy cross before to guide me.

5 And so through all the length of days
  Thy goodness faileth never;
  Good shepherd, may I sing thy praise
  Within thy house for ever!

Sir Henry Baker

1 Colours of day dawn into the mind,
  The sun has come up, the night is behind.
  Go down in the city, into the street,
  And let's give the message to the people we meet.

Chorus:
So light up the fire and let the flame burn,
Open the door, let Jesus return.
Take seeds of his Spirit, let the fruit grow,
Tell the people of Jesus, let his love show.

2 Go through the park, on into the town;
  The sun still shines on, it never goes down.
  The light of the world is risen again;
  The people of darkness are needing our friend.
Chorus

3 Open your eyes, look into the sky,
  The darkness has come, the sun came to die.
  The evening draws on, the sun disappears,
  But Jesus is living, his Spirit is near.
  Chorus

  Susan McClellan, John Pac and Keith Ryecroft

1 The Lord's my shepherd, I'll not want;
  He makes me down to lie
  In pastures green; He leadeth me
  The quiet waters by.

2 My soul He doth restore again,
  And me to walk doth make
  Within the paths of righteousness,
  E'en for His own name's sake.

3 Yea, though I walk in death's dark vale,
  Yet will I fear no ill;
  For thou art with me, and thy rod
  And staff me comfort still.

4 Goodness and mercy all my life
  Shall surely follow me,
  And in God's house for evermore
  My dwelling-place shall be.
                              Scottish Psalter

1 Think of all the things we lose,
  So many things, I get confused:
  Our pencil sharpeners, favourite books,
  Our indoor shoes and outdoor boots,
  Pocket money down the drain,
  Then felt-tip pens and people's names.
  The worst of all things to be lost
  Is just a friend you really trust.

2 Think of all the things we find,
So many things I bring to mind:
In lofts and cupboards, if you browse,
Are old tin whistles, acting clothes,
Clocks that used to chime, and bits
Of engines and of building kits:
But even better, I believe,
Is just a friend to share them with.

3 Think of times we lose our nerves,
We're feeling sad and no-one cares:
An empty feeling deep inside,
There's nowhere else for us to hide.
That's the time to call a friend
Whom we can never lose again:
There's one friend who is very near,
A friend who takes away our fear.
                    Tom McGuinness (adapted)

1 At the name of Jesus
Every knee shall bow,
Every tongue confess him
King of glory now;
'Tis the Father's pleasure
We should call him Lord,
Who from the beginning
Was the mighty Word.

2 Humbled for a season,
To receive a name
From the lips of sinners
Unto whom he came,
Faithfully he bore it
Spotless to the last,
Brought it back victorious
When from death he passed.

3 Name him, brothers, name him,
  With love as strong as death,
  But with awe and wonder,
  And with bated breath;
  He is God and Saviour,
  He is Christ the Lord,
  Ever to be worshipped,
  Trusted and adored.

4 In your hearts enthrone him;
  There let him subdue
  All that is not holy,
  All that is not true:
  Crown him as your captain
  In temptation's hour;
  Let his will enfold you
  In its light and power.

  Caroline Noel

59

Chorus:
I will bring to you the best gift I can offer;
I will sing to you the best things in my mind.

1 Paper pictures, bits of string, I'll bring you
  almost anything,
  I'll bring a song that only I can sing:
  The rainbow colours in the sky, the misty moon
  that caught my eye,
  The magic of a new-born butterfly.
  Chorus

2 I'll bring a song of winter trees, the skidding ice,
  the frozen leaves,
  The battles in our snowball-shouting streets.
  I'll bring you summers I have known, adventure
  trips and journeys home,
  The summer evenings playing down our road.
  Chorus

50

3 I'll share my secrets and my dreams, I'll show
   you wonders I have seen,
   And I will listen when you speak your name;
   And if you really want me to, I will share my
   friends with you,
   Everyone at home and in my school.
   Chorus

                                    Tom McGuinness

1 In the morning early
   I go down to the sea
   And see the mist on the shore;
   I listen, and I listen.

2 When I go to the rocks
   I go looking for shells
   And feel the sand beneath my feet;
   I listen, and I listen.

3 When the stormy day comes
   Waves crash on the cliffs
   And the wind whistles through my hair;
   I listen, and I listen.

4 And at night when I sleep
   And the sea is calm
   The gentle waves lap the shore;
   I listen, and I listen.

5 I sometimes think that God
   Is talking to me
   When I hear the sound of the sea;
   I listen, and I listen.
   I listen, and I listen.

                                    Hazel Charlton

61

1 All over the world,
Everywhere,
Where the sun shines,
And where the white snow gleams;
In the green, green forests and by the streams,
Hands are busy, plans are laid,
And slowly, slowly,
Somewhere, somebody's house is made.

Chorus:
Everybody's building, everybody's building,
Everybody's building, day by day,
Everybody's building, everybody's building,
Everybody's building in a different way.

2 All over the world,
Everywhere,
Where the sun shines,
And where the darkest night
Holds back the coming of the morning light:
Bricks are laid and wood is sawn,
And slowly, slowly,
Out of a dream a house is born.
Chorus

3 All over the world,
Everywhere,
Where we're living,
Wherever children grow,
And their lives are shaped as the moments go,
Minds are building, plans are laid,
And slowly, slowly,
Somewhere somebody's life is made.
Chorus

4 All over the world,
Everywhere,
Where we're living,
Wherever children play,
For the things they do and the things they say,
For good or ill, ground is laid,
And slowly, slowly,
Somewhere, somebody's life is made.
Chorus   David Winter

62

1 Heavenly Father, may thy blessing
Rest upon thy children now,
When in praise thy name they hallow,
When in prayer to thee they bow;
In the wondrous story reading
Of the Lord of truth and grace,
May they see thy love reflected
In the light of his dear face.

2 May they learn from this great story
All the arts of friendliness;
Truthful speech and honest action,
Courage, patience, steadfastness;
How to master self and temper,
How to make their conduct fair;
When to speak and when be silent,
When to do and when forbear.

3 May his spirit wise and holy
With his gifts their spirits bless,
Make them loving, joyous, peaceful,
Rich in goodness, gentleness,
Strong in self-control, and faithful,
Kind in thought and deed; for he
Sayeth, 'What ye do for others
Ye are doing unto me.'
William Charter-Piggott

53

Chorus:
Spirit of God, as strong as the wind,
Gentle as is the dove,
Give us your joy, and give us your peace,
Show to us Jesus' love.

1 You inspired men, long, long ago,
They then proclaimed your word;
We see their lives, serving mankind:
Through them your voice is heard.
Chorus

2 Without your help, we fail our Lord,
   We cannot live His way,
   We need your power, we need your strength,
   Following Christ each day.
   Chorus

Margaret Old
adapted by Geoffrey Marshall-Taylor

1 The wise may bring their learning,
   The rich may bring their wealth,
   And some may bring their greatness,
   And some their strength and health:
   We too would bring our treasures
   To offer to the King;
   We have no wealth or learning,
   What gifts then shall we bring?

2 We'll bring the many duties
   We have to do each day;
   We'll try our best to please Him,
   At home, at school, at play:
   And better are these treasures
   To offer to the King,
   Than richest gifts without them;
   Yet these we all may bring.

3 We'll bring Him hearts that love Him,
   We'll bring Him thankful praise,
   And lives for ever striving
   To follow in His ways:
   And these shall be the treasures
   We offer to the King,
   And these are gifts that ever
   Our grateful hearts may bring.

Book of Praise for Children (adapted)

1 When I needed a neighbour, were you there,
were you there?
When I needed a neighbour, were you there?

Chorus:
And the creed and the colour and the name
won't matter,
Were you there?

2 I was hungry and thirsty, were you there,
were you there?
I was hungry and thirsty, were you there?
Chorus

3 I was cold, I was naked, were you there,
were you there?
I was cold, I was naked, were you there?
Chorus

4 When I needed a shelter, were you there,
were you there?
When I needed a shelter, were you there?
Chorus

5 When I needed a healer, were you there,
were you there?
When I needed a healer, were you there?
Chorus

6 Wherever you travel, I'll be there, I'll be there,
Wherever you travel, I'll be there.

Chorus:
And the creed and the colour and the name
won't matter,
I'll be there.

Sydney Carter

1 In Christ there is no east or west,
In him no south or north,
But one great fellowship of love
Throughout the whole wide earth.

2 In him shall true hearts everywhere
Their high communion find;
His service is the golden cord
Close-binding all mankind.

3 Join hands, then, brothers of the faith,
Whate'er your race may be!
Who serves my Father as a son
Is surely kin to me.

4 In Christ now meet both east and west,
In him meet south and north;
All Christly souls are one in him,
Throughout the whole wide earth.
John Oxenham

1 The ink is black, the page is white,
Together we learn to read and write,
   to read and write;
And now a child can understand
This is the law of all the land,
   all the land;
The ink is black, the page is white,
Together we learn to read and write,
   to read and write.

2 The slate is black, the chalk is white,
The words stand out so clear and bright,
   so clear and bright;
And now at last we plainly see
The alphabet of liberty,
   liberty;
The slate is black, the chalk is white,
Together we learn to read and write,
   to read and write.

3 A child is black, a child is white,
  The whole world looks upon the sight,
    upon the sight;
  For very well the whole world knows,
  This is the way that freedom grows,
    freedom grows;
  A child is black, a child is white,
  Together we learn to read and write,
    to read and write.

4 The world is black, the world is white,
  It turns by day and then by night,
    and then by night;
  It turns so each and every one
  Can take his station in the sun,
    in the sun;
  The world is black, the world is white,
  Together we learn to read and write,
    to read and write.

David Arkin

1 Kum ba yah, my Lord, Kum ba yah,
  Kum ba yah, my Lord, Kum ba yah,
  Kum ba yah, my Lord, Kum ba yah,
  O Lord, Kum ba yah.

2 Someone's crying, Lord, Kum ba yah,
  Someone's crying, Lord, Kum ba yah,
  Someone's crying, Lord, Kum ba yah,
  O Lord, Kum ba yah.

3 Someone's singing, Lord, Kum ba yah,
  Someone's singing, Lord, Kum ba yah,
  Someone's singing, Lord, Kum ba yah,
  O Lord, Kum ba yah.

4 Someone's praying, Lord, Kum ba yah,
  Someone's praying, Lord, Kum ba yah,
  Someone's praying, Lord, Kum ba yah,
  O Lord, Kum ba yah.

Traditional

69

1 I belong to a family, the biggest on earth,
Ten thousand every day are coming to birth.
Our name isn't Davis or Groves or Jones,
It's the name every man should be proud he owns

Chorus:
It's the family of man, keeps growing,
The family of man, keeps sowing
The seeds of a new life every day.

2 I've got a sister in Melbourne, and brother
in Delhi,
The whole wide world is dad and mother to me.
Wherever you turn you will find my kin,
Whatever the creed or the colour of skin:
Chorus

3 The miner in the Rhondda, the coolie in Peking,
Men across the world who reap and plough
and spin,
They've got a life and others to share it,
Let's bridge the oceans and declare it:
Chorus

4 Some people say the world is a horrible place,
But it's just as good or bad as the human race;
Dirt and misery or health and joy,
Man can build or can destroy:
Chorus

Karl Dallas

1 Would you walk by on the other side,
When someone called for aid?
Would you walk by on the other side,
And would you be afraid?

Chorus:
Cross over the road, my friend,
Ask the Lord His strength to lend,
His compassion has no end,
Cross over the road.

2 Would you walk by on the other side,
When you saw a loved one stray?
Would you walk by on the other side,
Or would you watch and pray?
Chorus

3 Would you walk by on the other side,
When starving children cried?
Would you walk by on the other side
And would you not provide?
Chorus

Pamela Verrall

1 If I had a hammer, I'd hammer in the morning,
I'd hammer in the evening, all over this land;
I'd hammer out danger, I'd hammer out a
warning,
I'd hammer out love between my brothers
and my sisters,
All over this land.

2 If I had a bell, I'd ring it in the morning,
I'd ring it in the evening, all over this land;
I'd ring out danger, I'd ring out a warning,
I'd ring out love between my brothers
and my sisters,
All over this land.

3 If I had a song, I'd sing it in the morning,
  I'd sing it in the evening, all over this land;
  I'd sing out danger, I'd sing out a warning,
  I'd sing out love between my brothers
  and my sisters,
  All over this land.

4 Well, I've got a hammer, and I've got a bell,
  And I've got a song to sing all over this land;
  It's the hammer of justice, it's the bell of
  freedom,
  It's the song about love between my brothers
  and my sisters,
  All over this land.

Lee Hays

1 Every word comes alive,
  When it's written or read;
  There is life in a word,
  When it's sung or said.
  But there can't be a living word
  Never seen or never heard,
  But only when
  It gives itself
  To tongue and . . . pen!
      And a tune is alive
      When it's played or sung;
      It will even thrive
      Whistled, scraped or rung.
      Then it meets the word, and wakes;
      As you strike the notes, it breaks
      Into a living song.

2 But a song must grow
  In a singer too,
  And it needs to flow
  Into me and you.
  For it's lost and it can't be found
  If we never make it sound,
  So take a chance
  And lift the song to
  Make it . . . dance!

Now the word's in me,
And I make it shout,
And the tune rings free
As I peal it out.
And the words and the tune are one,
Singing me as I sing it on,
For I'm a living song.

Arthur Scholey

INDEX: page numbers (feint) and song numbers (bold).
Titles which are different from the first line
appear in italics.

A living song   60 **72**
A man for all the people   26 **27**
All creatures of our God and King   11 **7**
All over the world   52 **61**
All the nations of the earth   16 **14**
All things bright and beautiful   8 **3**
At the name of Jesus   49 **58**
Autumn days when the grass is jewelled   9 **4**
Black and white   56 **67**
Can you be sure that the rain will fall?   30 **31**
Carpenter, carpenter, make me a tree   9 **5**
Colours of day dawn into the mind   47 **55**
Come and praise the Lord our king   22 **21**
Come, my brothers, praise the Lord   21 **20**
Cross over the road   59 **70**
Every word comes alive   60 **72**
Father, hear the prayer we offer   43 **48**
Fill thou my life, O lord my God   37 **41**
Fill your hearts with joy and gladness   12 **9**
For the beauty of the earth   13 **11**
From the darkness came light   29 **29**
Give me oil in my lamp, keep me burning   39 **43**
Go, tell it on the mountain   24 **24**
God has promised   30 **31**
God is love   34 **36**
God knows me   17 **15**
God who made the earth   12 **10**
Have you heard the raindrops   7 **2**
He gave me eyes so I could see   20 **18**
He made me   20 **18**
He who would valiant be   40 **44**
He's got the whole world   20 **19**
Heavenly Father, may thy blessing   53 **62**
I belong to a family, the biggest on earth   58 **69**
I danced in the morning   22 **22**
I listen and I listen   51 **60**
I will bring to you the best gift I can offer   50 **59**
If I had a hammer, I'd hammer in the morning   59 **71**
In Christ there is no east or west   56 **66**
In the morning early   51 **60**
Jesus Christ is here   25 **26**

Jesus, good above all other   23 **23**
Join with us to sing God's praises   30 **30**
Judas and Mary   27 **28**
Kum ba yah, my Lord, Kum ba yah   57 **68**
Let us with a gladsome mind   11 **8**
Light up the fire   47 **55**
Lord of all hopefulness   45 **52**
Lord of the dance   22 **22**
Lost and found   48 **57**
Morning has broken   7 **1**
My faith it is an oaken staff   41 **46**
Now thank we all our God   35 **38**
O Lord, all the world belongs to you   36 **39**
O praise ye the Lord!   34 **37**
Oh praise Him!   14 **13**
One more step along the world I go   42 **47**
Our Father who art in heaven   45 **51**
Peace, perfect peace, is the gift of Christ our Lord   46 **53**
Praise Him   37 **40**
Praise the Lord in everything   32 **33**
Praise the Lord in the rhythm of your music   32 **33**
Praise the Lord, you heavens, adore Him   33 **35**
Praise to the Lord   32 **34**
Said Judas to Mary   27 **28**
Somebody greater   9 **5**
Song of Caedmon   14 **13**
Spirit of God, as strong as the wind   53 **63**
Thank you, Lord, for this new day   31 **32**
The best gift   50 **59**
The building song   52 **61**
The earth is yours, O God   10 **6**
The family of man   58 **69**
The ink is black, the page is white   56 **67**
The journey of life   40 **45**
The King of love my shepherd is   47 **54**
The Lord's my shepherd, I'll not want   48 **56**
The Lord's Prayer   45 **51**
The wise may bring their learning   54 **64**
There are hundreds of sparrows   17 **15**
There is singing in the desert   25 **26**
There's a child in the streets   26 **27**
Think of all the things we lose   48 **57**
Think of a world without any flowers   19 **17**

Travel on, travel on, there's a river that is flowing   38 **42**
Water of life   7 **2**
We are climbing Jesus' ladder   43 **49**
When a knight won his spurs in the stories of old   44 **50**
When God made the garden of creation   18 **16**
When I needed a neighbour   55 **65**
When Jesus walked in Galilee   25 **25**
Who put the colours in the rainbow?   14 **12**
Would you walk by on the other side   59 **70**